10 Minutes a Day
to Reading Success

activities and skill builders to help your first grader learn to love reading

Houghton Mifflin Company
Boston   New York   1998

3 06120W 3 9971

Product Development: Editorial Options, Inc.
Project Editor: Gari Fairweather
Designer: Lynne Torrey

Illustrations by Steve Henry
Pencil page spot art previously published in Houghton Mifflin's *Phonics, Books 1-5*, copyright
(c) 1997 by Houghton Mifflin Company. Pencil page art also by: Liz Callen, Roberta Holmes,
Susan Jaeckel, Jane McCreary, Ed Parker, Lou Vaccaro, Joe Veno

For information about permission to reproduce selections from this book, write to Permissions,
Houghton Mifflin Company, 215 Park Avenue South, New York, New York, 10003.

ISBN 0-395-90153-7

Printed in the United States of America

DOC 10 9 8 7 6 5 4 3 2 1

Table of Contents

Introduction

Getting Started

Your child is off to first grade! You're probably wondering what you can do to help your child succeed in school. If you're like most of today's busy adults, you're juggling several projects at a time and looking to focus on those things that will *really* be helpful.

How can you reinforce what your child is learning in school? One way is to let your child see you reading. When you read, your child sees that reading is a worthwhile activity. Another way is to read with your child. When you share a book, your child not only has a chance to practice his or her reading skills but also to feel close to you. You can also share many different kinds of activities that promote literacy and are fun to do. That's where this book comes in.

Using *10 Minutes a Day to Reading Success*

This book contains activities you and your child can do together to reinforce concepts and skills being taught in school. Some can be completed in as little as ten minutes. Others are a bit more involved. There is no correct time limit for completing an activity, however, since each child works at his or her own pace. Look for these icons as a general guide to the amount of time an activity might take:

 estimates the minutes required for an activity

 denotes activities requiring more than half an hour

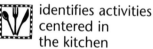 identifies activities centered in the kitchen

You'll find that activities with the kitchen icon make use of materials and staples found in your kitchen. Many of the other projects require materials readily found in most homes, such as crayons, markers, glue, scissors, paper, and index cards. Still other activities, like our pencil pages, invite your child to color and write in the book. Some of these pages can be completed independently, so if you need to step away for a minute, your child can continue without you.

You'll notice that the book is divided into thematic chapters designed to help your child acquire vocabulary and expand his or her knowledge base. Each chapter begins with a brief note to you that identifies the reading skills practiced in the chapter's activities. Look also for these icons, which provide information for parents, teachers, and other adults.

 Note explains a reading skill or suggests ways in which to complete an activity.

 Helping Hand provides tips for an activity, suggests alternative materials, or provides information of interest.

 More Ideas offers suggestions for other projects or ways to expand an especially enjoyable activity.

Each chapter includes a list of theme-related books you can share with your child. (You may want to gather these books early on, so you can enjoy them throughout a chapter.) At the end of each chapter is a story your child can read independently or with your help.

Feel free to photocopy or to cut up the pages. You can also use our pencil pages more than once. You might use them at the beginning of a chapter to determine how much your child already knows or use them at the end to find out how much your child has learned. Keep track of the activities your child completes by coloring in the circle at the bottom of each page.

About Learning to Read

Learning to read is a lot like learning to speak. It takes time, practice, and it's not always perfect the first time. Recall all the positive reinforcement you gave your child when he or she began to say words. Then apply this same enthusiasm, and patience, to learning to read.

Once children learn to hear the different sounds in words, they are ready to attach letters to those sounds. This is what phonics is all about. For example, children learn to associate the *p* sound at the beginning of *pet* with the letter *p*. This association will help children to read words that begin with *p* (*pet*), end with *p* (*top*), or begin with the *pl* cluster (*plop*). Children also learn to use common endings, or phonograms, to read words like *bet*, *get*, *jet*, and so on. For many children, learning sound-letter correspondences takes a lot of practice. That's where the activities and the pencil pages in this book can help. Playing word games and practicing sound-letter associations will help your child to develop the phonics skills needed to decode words.

Beginning readers also use context to help them read new words. The broader a child's vocabulary and world knowledge, the easier it will be for him or her to understand what is being read. That's why the activities in this book are theme based — to help develop needed vocabulary and concepts. Exploring new topics will help to expand your child's vocabulary and knowledge base as well.

The order in which you complete the activities in this book is up to you. You can work through one chapter, and then move on to the next. Or, you might skip around, choosing activities that appeal to your child. (Note: If your child's school uses Houghton Mifflin's reading/language arts program INVITATIONS TO LITERACY, there is a direct correspondence between the sequence of skills presented in that program and the sequence of the skills presented in this book.)

We hope you and your child will have fun. We know that finding time to do one more thing in a busy day is never easy. But by making the most of the time you do have—even ten minutes a day—you can make a big difference in your child's attitude toward reading!

In the Kitchen

Mix a Pancake

Mix a pancake,
Stir a pancake,
Pop it in the pan;
Fry the pancake,
Toss the pancake—
Catch it if you can.

Christina Rossetti

A Note About In the Kitchen

Besides being the place to prepare a favorite meal or recipe, the kitchen is a wonderful spot to help your child practice reading skills. That's why we chose *In the Kitchen* for our first chapter—and why *In the Kitchen* activities are included in all subsequent chapters. We begin with a brief introduction to the kitchen and a review of reading skills typically covered at the beginning of first grade. These include the following:

PHONICS/INITIAL AND FINAL CONSONANTS: Once a child knows the letters of the alphabet, he or she can begin to associate sounds with the letters. This chapter provides *lots* of practice with both beginning and ending sounds.

NOTING DETAILS: In a good picture book, the words tell only part of the story; the pictures tell the other part. Your child is learning to look for important details in a story's pictures—details that are critical to the story line. The color of a cook's apron might not be important to the story, for instance, but a picture of the cook's knocking an ingredient off the table might be *very* important.

CATEGORIZE/CLASSIFY: We use this important thinking skill every day, yet it's hard to remember when or how we first learned it. Invite your child to help you do sorting and putting-away tasks around the house. Talk about *why* you group certain things together, and ask your child to suggest other ways to group things.

In addition to the above reading skills, first graders are learning important reading strategies. One such strategy is *making predictions.* Can your child guess what a book might be about based on its title and cover illustration? While reading with your child, stop every now and then to predict what might happen next. You and your child can practice this strategy together the next time you watch your favorite television show, too. It's a great way to spend commercial-break time.

Introduce *In the Kitchen* and the playful dog mascot for this book by sharing the poem on page 7. Read the rhyme aloud, inviting your child to chime in on any familiar words. Then invite your child to read the poem aloud.

Who's Coming to Dinner?

If you were having guests for dinner, how might you prepare? Here are some ideas. Choose one or do all three!

🕐 Napkin Rings

Save the cardboard tube from a paper towel roll. Ask a grownup to cut the tube into two-inch rings. Color the rings with bright magic markers, and let them dry. Then, roll up a napkin and place it inside the ring. Now you have a napkin ring for each place setting.

🕐 Name Cards

Cut out squares of heavy paper. Fold each square in half so it opens and closes like a greeting card. Turn the card so that it opens toward you, and then write a guest's name on the top flap. You can also add a drawing. Place a name card by each place setting.

🕐 Place Mats

Decorate large pieces of drawing paper to make place mats for everyone at your table. You can draw your guests' favorite things. Be sure to include each person's name on his or her place mat. You can even make a place mat for a pet!

💡 To make place mats last, laminate them. Sheets of laminating material can be purchased in stationery stores, drug stores, or supermarkets.

📝 Watch as your child connects the alphabet dots on the following pencil page. If your child falters, say the alphabet together. For more practice, make an alphabet strip so that your child can practice saying the letters in order.

ABC
Connect-the-Dots

Who else is coming to dinner?
Say your ABC's and connect
the dots to find out!

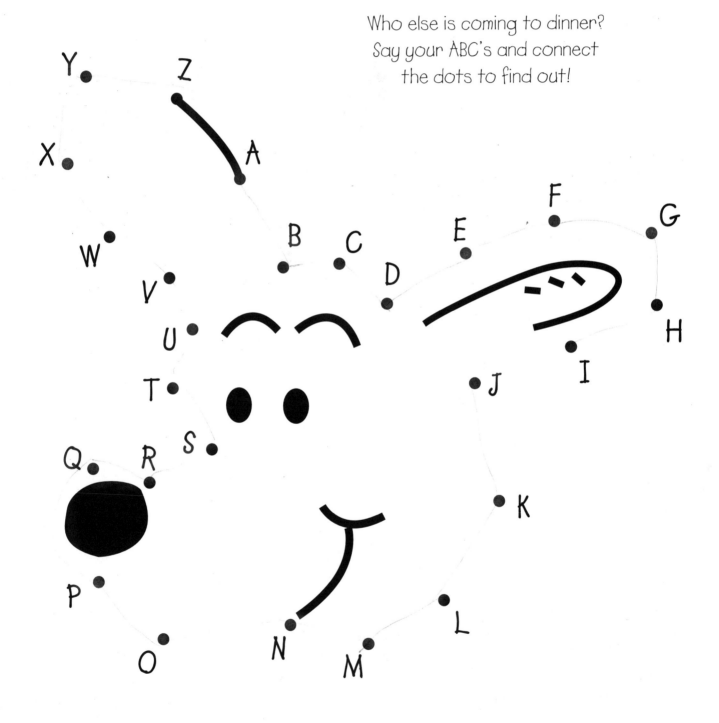

Kitchen Words

How many things in your kitchen can you name? Take turns with someone else naming objects that catch your eye. Set a time limit and try not to name the same thing twice.

 ## Label It!

Let's really get to know your kitchen. Use sticky notes or index cards to make labels for the things you just named. For each label, do this:

• Say the name of the object. What letter stands for the beginning sound?

After a while, take down the labels and use them as word cards. Save your child's word cards in a word box.

Labeling is an important beginning reading activity. It helps develop sight vocabulary, words a child recognizes right away. While making labels with your child, notice the beginning and ending sounds your child identifies. If he or she has trouble with a particular letter sound, use the activities in this chapter to practice it.

• Write the word on a note. (A grownup can help you with the spelling.)

• Draw a picture for each label.

Now you can stick the labels on their matching objects all around your kitchen and practice reading the words each day.

Dough Letters

Try this dough recipe to cook up some fun! Remember, dough can be messy, so wear old clothes. Make sure you have an adult helping you.

Homemade Dough

You'll need:
- 2 cups flour
- 1/2 cup salt
- 3/4 cup hot tap water
- 1 medium bowl

- Mix the flour and salt in a medium bowl. Ask a grownup to add the hot water and stir the mixture for you. Then knead the dough on a floured surface for five minutes until it becomes easy to shape. (Hint: A teaspoon of vegetable oil will make the dough smoother.)

- Take a small handful of dough and shape it into a letter. Can you make all the letters in your name?

- Spell out your name or a few of your favorite words.

- Make a short word, like **cat**. Change the first letter to spell a new word like **bat**. How many other words can you make?

You can use the dough to roll out necklace beads, too. Air drying takes one to five days. Small shapes can be dried more quickly by baking them on a cookie sheet at 200° for about two hours. Dried items can be painted with poster paints. Instead of painting, you can also add food coloring during the kneading process.

The activities on pages 13, 15, and 17 provide practice with beginning consonant sounds. After your child completes the pages, read the words aloud together.

Beginning Sounds

s m t p c n

Name the picture. What letter is missing?

_____ op

_____ an

_____ ix

_____ up

_____ ine

_____ op

Picture Names: _mop, pan, six, cup, nine, top_

13

Eating the Alphabet

🕐 It's time to pretend you are a famous chef and stir up some make-believe alphabet soup! You can use magnetic letters, Scrabble® squares, or letter cards to make words. A big spoon comes in handy for this project.

The cat sat on my hat.

Play with Your Food!

Here are some games to play while you "eat" the alphabet meal you've made:

- Scoop up a letter and name it. Then name some words that begin with the sound for that letter.

- Scoop up a letter, but don't name it. Say words that begin with the sound for that letter, and have someone else guess the letter.

- Spell out a short word like **cat** or **pig**. Then name words that end with the same rhyming sounds, like **hat** or **wig**. Can you think of some silly sentences using the rhyming words?

📋 Try some of these games with alphabet shaped foods such as noodles, soup, or cereal. Watch out—this can get messy! Or, take the game on the road with dry alphabet cereal.

📋 As your child completes the activities on pages 15 and 17, watch for beginning letter-sound associations that might need more practice.

More Beginning Sounds

r b j k f g

Name each picture and write the missing letter.

____ey

____ear

____ar

____ish

____oat

____ing

Picture Names: *key, bear, jar, fish, goat, ring*

15

My Shopping List

The next time you go shopping for groceries, try these activities to turn your trip into an adventure.

Making a List... Checking It Twice

People often make lists to remember things. A grocery list is a good reminder for a shopper. Here are some fun grocery lists you can use:

- Ask a grownup to write a mystery list by leaving a blank for the first letter in each item. As you shop, fill in the beginning letter.

- Help gather coupons from newspapers and magazines. Use the coupons as a shopping list to help you hunt for items with a grownup.

- Be prepared! Keep a pad of paper and a pencil in your kitchen. Each time something is used up, add it to the list for the next trip.

_ilk
_ananas
_ettuce
_amburger
_omatoes
_uns

A grocery store is a great place to help your child associate a spoken word with its written form. As you shop, ask your child to look for familiar labels. Find packaged foods that have words and pictures on the labels that your child can read.

Still More Beginning Sounds

d h v w l y

You know what to do! Write the missing letter in each word.

_____agon

_____est

_____ook

_____arn

_____oor

_____amp

Picture Names: *wagon, vest, hook, yarn, door, lamp*

My Picture Dictionary

Do you know what a kiwi looks like? How about a zucchini? One place you could find out is a picture dictionary. Here's how you can create your own.

Things We Eat

Begin your dictionary by looking for pictures of food in old magazines. Cut out the foods you find and sort them by beginning sounds. Put **pears** with **pies**, for example.

Next, choose one letter and design a picture dictionary page for it.

1) Write the letter at the top of the page.

2) Place the pictures that begin with the sound for that letter on the page, and then glue the pictures in place.

3) Label the pictures, or ask someone to help you write out the picture names.

For a first dictionary page, pick a letter like *p*, which introduces a variety of foods, such as *peach, pear, plum, pineapple, peas, pumpkin, pizza, pretzel, pie,* and *popsicle.* Or, choose a letter for which your child needs extra practice.

Keep the pages in a three-ring binder. As the dictionary grows, use tabbed dividers to identify and separate letters. As your child clips pictures, store them until he or she is ready to make a new dictionary page.

Packing a Picnic Basket

Most picnics begin in the kitchen. Part of the fun is planning what to take. Here's how to play a game about packing for a **make-believe** picnic:

How to Play

First, find someone (or several someones) to play the game with you. Then, do this:

- Choose a consonant letter, like **t**.

- Take turns saying words that begin with that letter to finish the sentence: "I'm packing a picnic basket and I'm taking **toast** and **tomatoes**."

- Play until no one can think of another picnic word that begins with that letter.

- Then play with another consonant.

More Ways to Play

Here are other ways to pack for a make-believe picnic:

- Repeat the items other players say before adding your own.

- Add things in order from **A** to **Z**.

- Add things that end with the same sound and letter: **top, cap, cup.**

This great game can help you determine which consonants your child knows and which ones he or she needs more practice on. If your child has trouble thinking of words for a particular consonant, make a picture dictionary page for that letter. (See page 18.) This game is fun for road trips, too.

Just Desserts

What comes at the end of a meal? Dessert, of course! A meal has a beginning and an end, just like a word. Here are two word games to play while eating dessert.

Bite by Bite

This game makes your dessert last longer because you eat as you play. Ask someone to play with you. Then, do this:

- Choose a consonant letter. How about **d**?

- Before you take a bite of dessert, name a word that **ends** with the sound for that letter, like **bread**.

- Take turns naming letters and words. Maybe the person who comes up with the most words can get another dessert!

Front or Back

Play "Front or Back" while you help clear the table.

- Choose a consonant letter, like **l**.

- Ask a grownup to name words that **begin** or **end** with this letter—like **lamp, ball, meal**.

- Say "front" or "back" to tell where you hear the sound for that letter.

The pencil pages that follow provide practice with ending sounds. If your child has difficulty, say each picture name aloud, emphasizing the sound for the final letter.

The first few times you play "Bite by Bite," your child might have difficulty suggesting words that end with a particular letter sound. If this is the case, suggest two words—such as *bed/bell*—and ask your child to name the one that ends with the chosen consonant sound.

Ending Sounds

Name the pictures. Write the ending letter to complete each word.

k p r g t d

ca____

ca____

boo____

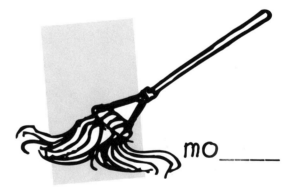

mo____

be____

pi____

Picture Names: *cat, car, book, mop, bed, pig*

21

More Ending Sounds

n l s m b f x

Write the ending letter to complete each word.

si____

su____

tu____

dru____

whee____

bu____

lea____

Picture Names: *six, sun, tub, drum, wheel, bus, leaf*

Where in the Kitchen?

Take a look around your kitchen. Where would you look to find a spoon? Some milk? A can of soup? How about your socks? Oops, wrong room!

Sort It Out

Look for other ways items are sorted. You might check in the drawers, cabinets, and closets of your home. Or, take your search on the road and look for ways items are sorted at the:

- supermarket,
- hardware store,
- drug store,
- library.

Sorting is an important thinking skill used throughout your child's school years. You can help your child by providing many opportunities for sorting, such as sorting laundry, matching socks, or grouping toys. Help him or her to sort items by color, size, texture, and use.

Everything Has a Place

Most people like to group things together. You may keep silverware in a drawer and dishes in a cabinet. In a drawer, silverware may be sorted into even smaller groups—forks, spoons, knives.

Sorting can be a fun way to help in the kitchen. You can:

- Sort and put away silverware or foods for the cupboard (watch out for sharp knives).
- Sort foods for the refrigerator and freezer.

Kitchen Garden

Do you have a green thumb? Try one of these ideas to grow plants in your kitchen.

Carrots in a Tub

The next time you have carrots for dinner, save the carrot tops. Leave only an inch of the orange part. Set the tops in a dish of water. In a few days, little roots will appear. Fill an empty butter or margarine tin with soil and plant the carrot tops. Keep the soil moist. In about a week, curly greens will sprout.

Beans in a Jar

Line an empty jar with a paper towel. Place a few lima beans between the towel and the glass. Add water, a little at a time, until the towel is wet. Put the jar in a warm, dark place. Check the towel every day, and add more water as needed to keep it wet. In a few days, your beans will sprout.

Observe the plants on a daily basis with your child and keep a record of each plant's growth. Your child can draw pictures to show what the plants look like and dictate sentences about the plants for you to write. This is a great way to practice noting details and to develop observation skills.

Avocado in a Jar

Save the pit from an avocado and let it dry for a day or two. Then remove the brown skin from the pit. Poke three toothpicks into the pit and rest it, pointy end up, in a jar of water. The bottom of the pit should be in the water.

Check the pit every day to see if it needs more water. In a few weeks, a root will appear. Then plant your avocado in a flowerpot. Watch it grow!

Potato in a Glass

With toothpicks, rest a sweet potato or a regular potato in a glass. Add water so that half of the potato is covered. Check the glass every day to see if you need to add more water. Soon roots and sprouts will grow. The sprouts will turn into a leafy, green vine.

chen Concentration

When you're not cooking or eating in the kitchen, try this *memory game*.

◑ Get Ready

Make letter cards for both capital and lowercase letters (See page 27). Then look back at a pencil page on beginning sounds (See pages 13, 15, and 17). Take out the capital and lowercase cards for the letters on one pencil page.

Play with a Partner

To play with a partner, do this:

1) Set up the cards, face down.

2) Take turns turning over two cards until you make a capital and lowercase letter match.

3) If you make a match, name a word that begins with that letter to keep the cards. If not, turn the cards back over.

4) The player who matches the most cards wins!

Play Alone

You can play by yourself, like this:

1) Mix up the letter cards. Then place them face down in rows.

2) Turn over two letter cards at a time and try to make a capital and lowercase letter match, like **B** and **b**.

3) If you make a match, keep the cards. If not, turn the cards back over.

4) Play until you've matched all the cards.

For an added challenge, name a word that ends with a letter sound to make a match.

You can copy and cut apart the following pencil page to make letter cards. Or, trace the squares for your child and ask him or her to trace the letters.

Letter Cards

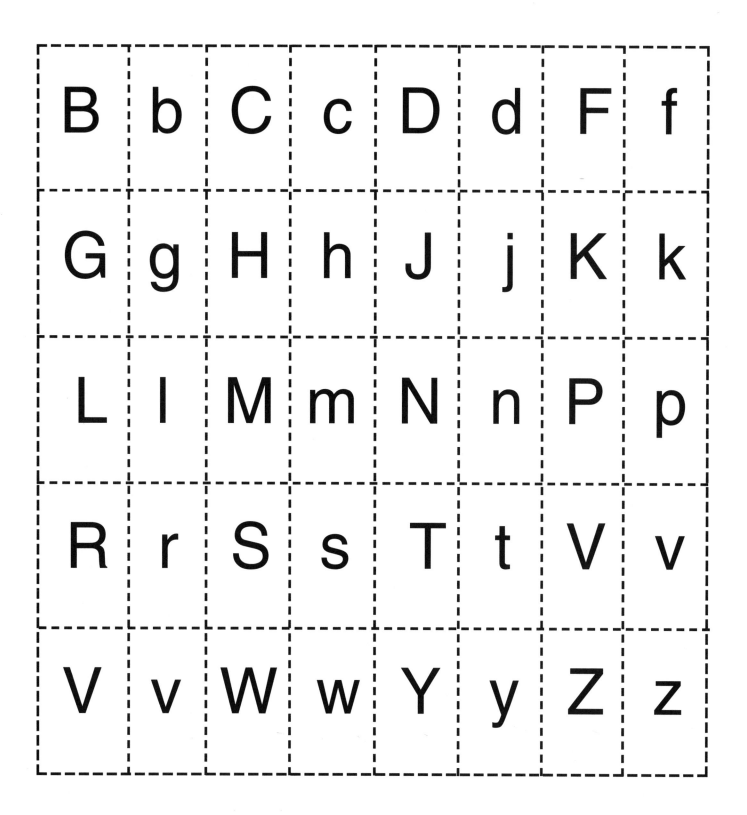

B	b	C	c	D	d	F	f
G	g	H	h	J	j	K	k
L	l	M	m	N	n	P	p
R	r	S	s	T	t	V	v
V	v	W	w	Y	y	Z	z

Books to Share

Help your child to find some of these books at the library by explaining that picture books are grouped in alphabetical order by the author's last name.

Eating the Alphabet: Fruits and Vegetables from A to Z by Lois Ehlert (Harcourt, 1989). At least one fruit or vegetable appears for each letter in this ABC book.

Green Eggs and Ham by Dr. Seuss (Random House, 1960). In this Dr. Seuss classic, Sam-I-Am tries to convince a companion to eat a plate of green eggs and ham.

Pie's in the Oven by Betty G. Birney (Houghton Mifflin, 1996). Your child can use this book to practice making predictions. Use the title and the cover illustration to predict what the story is about.

Pancakes for Breakfast by Tomie dePaola (Harcourt, 1978). In this wordless book, picture details let your child tell the story. Talk about the use of thought balloons and labels on the ingredients.

More books you might enjoy:

Daddy Makes the Best Spaghetti by Anna Grossnickle Hines (Clarion, 1986). Daily routines become games as Corey helps Daddy cook and Mommy clean up.

Jamberry by Bruce Degen (Harper, 1983). A boy and a bear go berry picking in this rollicking adventure.

Curious George and the Pizza by Margaret Rey and Allan Shalleck (Houghton Mifflin, 1988). Everyone's favorite monkey is up to his elbows in dough—and trouble.

Martha Blah Blah by Susan Meddaugh (Houghton Mifflin, 1996). Martha, the talking dog, can no longer speak.

 Suggestions

Invite your child to read aloud the story on the next page. Point out that the underlined words may be new. Remind your child to think about the sounds of letters and picture clues.

✱ After reading the fourth frame, ask how the story might end. Then read the last page together to check your predictions.

✱ Your child can use the language pattern from the story to write about his or her favorite pizza. For example: "I like olives on my pizza," said Rita.

Time for Dinner

1

"I like <u>tomatoes</u>," said the cat.
"I like <u>mushrooms</u>," said the dog.

2

"I like <u>sausage</u>," said the cat.
"I like <u>pepperoni</u>," said the dog.

3

"I like <u>peppers</u>," said the cat.
"I like <u>beans</u>," said the dog.

4

"I like <u>peas</u>," said the cat.
"I like <u>corn</u>," said the dog.

5

"We like <u>pizza</u>!" said the cat and the dog.

6

Draw and write about a pizza you like.

"I like _____ on my pizza!" said _____.

Family Fun

The Joke

The joke you just told isn't funny one bit.
It's pointless and dull, wholly lacking in wit.
It's so old and stale, it's beginning to smell!
Besides, it's the one I was going to tell.

Anonymous

A Note About Family Fun

First graders know that learning takes place in school. But another truth is that the more experiences children bring to the classroom, the better prepared and able they are to learn. Everything a child sees and does adds to his or her understanding of the world. And, since a child's early experiences are most often shared with family, we've included a chapter packed with family fun that also practices the following reading skills:

PHONICS/CONSONANT CLUSTERS: After learning the sounds that single consonants represent, first graders are introduced to consonant clusters, two or more consonant letters whose sounds are blended together in a word. In this chapter, your child will practice consonant clusters with *r, l,* and *s.*

PHONICS/CONSONANT DIGRAPHS: Once children have grasped letter and sound correspondences, they are introduced to digraphs, letters that form a single new sound when joined together. This chapter practices the digraphs *sh, th,* and *ch.*

NOTING DETAILS: In *Family Fun*, your child continues to practice noting details. In addition to helping your child comprehend a story, noting details can help him or her to read unfamiliar words.

SEQUENCE: Most children are introduced to sequence through the alphabet and numbers. They then learn order words, such as *first, next,* and *last,* that define steps in a process. This, in turn, prepares youngsters to recognize that stories also have a sequence. *Family Fun* explores sequence through family stories and experiences.

One important reading strategy young readers learn to use is integrated word analysis or, more simply, they learn to *think about words.* When your child is reading and comes across an unfamiliar word, encourage him or her to try and figure out the word using one or more of these approaches:

- think about consonant and vowel sounds to decode the word;
- look for familiar word parts to decode the word;
- think about what makes sense in the sentence to read the word or learn its meaning;
- look at illustrations for clues to the word or its meaning.

Family Pictures

What did you look like last year? Was your hair long or short? Were you missing any teeth? One way to find out is to look at family pictures.

◔ Photo Detective

Look at family photographs with a grownup. How have you changed since last year? What's the same? How are other family members the same or different?

Be a detective. Look closely for details that tell more about the picture. When was it taken? Where? A cake might tell you it's someone's birthday, for instance. Which picture do you like the most?

◑ Making a Picture Frame

People treasure family pictures because they are reminders of special times. Draw a picture of an event you'd like to remember. Then make a frame for your new picture.

- Ask a grownup to help you cut out the center of a piece of cardboard (The hole should be about an inch smaller than the picture).

- Decorate the frame with stickers, glitter, or foil.

- Place the frame over your picture and tape it into place. Then display your new family treasure!

Cardboard from a cereal box makes a good frame. Use the extra cardboard piece to back the picture. Or, have your child draw the picture in the center of a paper plate and decorate the rim.

My Home Video

Do you like videos? Home movies? Here's an idea for making your own home video! You'll need shelf paper for the "film" and a big box for the "TV."

Create a TV

Here's how to make the TV. Ask a grownup to help you with any cutting:

1) Cut a large square in the bottom of the box for the TV "screen."

2) Cut a slit down opposite sides of the box. The slits should be a little wider than the shelf paper.

3) Decorate your TV with knobs, dials, or buttons.

Produce a Video

What family story would you like to share? How about a family trip? List some of your ideas. Then choose a story for your video. Draw pictures to show what happened **first, next,** and **last**. Add more pictures if you want.

To watch your video, pull the shelf paper through the slits. Tell the story as you show the pictures.

Sequencing events is an important reading and writing skill. Help your child order story events and encourage the use of order words—*first, next, then,* and *last*—as he or she narrates the video.

• To space the scenes on the shelf paper, mark off drawing frames the size of the "TV screen."
• In lieu of shelf paper, use fax paper rolls, continuous-feed computer paper, or sheets of paper taped together.

The following pencil page provides practice with *r* clusters, such as *trip*. Other r clusters are *br, cr, dr, fr, gr,* and *pr*. What other r cluster words can your child name?

Clusters with r

Color **green** the pictures that begin with **gr**. Color **brown** those that begin with **br**. What picture do you see? What letters spell the beginning sounds?

Picture Names: *grass, grapes, frog, brush, drum, broom, crayon, pretzel, bread, tray*
Answer: *tree*

35

Gone Fishing

How would you like to go on a family fishing trip? You can with this fishing game, and you don't even have to leave the house!

Get Ready

To go fishing you'll need a fishing rod and some paper fish. Here's how:

- To make a fishing rod, tie a piece of string to the end of a stick. Then tie a magnet to the other end of the string.

- Cut out your fish from colored paper. Write a letter pair on each fish: **bl, cl, fl, gl, pl,** and **sl**. Put a paper clip on the "mouth" of each fish.

Go Fishing!

- Scatter the fish on the floor and dangle your line over them. What happens when the magnet touches a paper clip? That's right, you catch a fish!

- Now look at the letters on the fish. Can you name a word that begins with the sounds for those letters? Take turns naming words with your fishing partner. When you can't think of any more words, go fishing again.

If your child has trouble naming *l* cluster words, suggest two words for him or her to choose from. For example: Does *bl* stand for the sound at the beginning of *blue* or *brown*?

Adapt the activity to practice other consonant clusters, to review single consonant letter sounds, or to practice sight words.

Clusters with l

bl cl fl gl pl sl

Name each picture.
Write the missing
letters.

_____ower

_____ed

_____ove

_____ock

_____ate

_____ock

_____ag

Picture Names: *flower, sled, glove, clock, plate, block, flag*

Family Sports

Do you have a favorite sport? How about soccer? Maybe you like to swim or skate. Think of the things you and your family like to do for fun.

◑ Sports Star Mobile

- Invite family members to talk about activities and sports they enjoy. Make a list of the different activities. Be sure to include the things you like, too.

- Then, ask a grownup to help you cut out several large stars from construction paper. Create a sports star for each person in your family. Write the word for the sport on one side. Write the name of the person who likes that sport on the other side.

- Poke a hole in each star and hang it from a hanger with string.

Many sports and activities use the "ing" form of a word, like *swimming*. Your child, however, might find it easier to sound out and write the base word, *swim*.

Together, revisit the list of activities and sports to see how many begin with consonant clusters. With *s* clusters? More practice with *s* clusters is provided on the following pencil pages.

Clusters with s

sk sl sn sw

Name each picture. Write the missing letters. Hint: each begins with s.

_____ate

_____ide

_____eakers

_____im

_____ed

_____ing

_____is

Picture Names: _skate, slide, sneakers, sled, swim, swing, skis_

39

More Clusters with s

sc sm sp st

Here are some more **s** words. Can you write the missing letters?

_____arf

_____apler

_____ider

_____ile

_____ale

_____ar

_____ock

Picture Names: *scarf, stapler, spider, smile, scale, star, smock*

Do you have a family member or friend who lives far away? Here are some fun ways to keep in touch.

Family Pen Pal

Postcards

Use a big index card to create a homemade postcard. Illustrate the front of the card with a picture of something you've seen or done recently. On the other side, write a short message and sign your name. Ask a grownup to help you address and stamp the postcard. Then mail it.

Dear Nana,
Please Come
visit!
Love, Alex

Mrs. Anders
14 Tulip Street
New City, Florida

Puzzle Surprise

Draw a picture and write a message on it. Cut the drawing into puzzle pieces. Put the pieces in an envelope and mail them. In a few days, your special someone will have a puzzle to solve and a letter to read!

E-mail

What is e-mail? It's electronic mail that travels quickly over telephone lines to a friend or family member. In fact, e-mail is so fast that stamped mail has a new nickname, "snail mail."

Many children aren't keen on letter writing until they start receiving their own mail. Consider asking a friend or family member to initiate a pen pal relationship with your child.

Friends or family members subscribing to the same internet provider can often send instant messages to one another. Help your child carry on such on-line conversations.

Lunch 'N' Munch Fun

Lunch at Lee's
Thursday, 12 o'clock
Menu
Ham and Cheese Roll-ups
Thick Vanilla Shakes

You can have lots of family fun in the kitchen. Here are a few ideas to spice up your next lunch.

Lunch Menu

Ask a grownup to help you plan an invitation menu for a friend to come to lunch. The menu should tell the time of the lunch and what you'll serve.

Shapely Sandwiches

To dress up a peanut butter and jelly sandwich, use a cookie cutter to stamp out a fun sandwich shape

Finger Sandwiches

Make your favorite sandwich, but don't cut it in half. Cut it into thin, finger-sized strips.

Ham & Cheese Roll-Ups

Place a piece of ham on top of a slice of cheese. Roll up the pieces for a fun sandwich that doesn't need any bread. Stick a toothpick in it to hold it together.

With your child, look through newspapers and store circulars for pictures of foods that begin or end with consonant clusters, like *grapes* or *bread*. Cut out the pictures and use them to create meal-time menus.

"Help Out" Plans

Families play together, and they also work together. When everyone helps out, the work goes faster.

How Can I Help?

Some chores are big. Some are small. But little jobs can add up to be a big help. With a grownup, list projects you can do around the house. Divide the list into big and little jobs. Then make a "Help-Out Chart."

- Little Helps are jobs you do every day, like make your bed, get ready for school, feed a pet, and put dirty clothes in the hamper.

- Big Helps are jobs you might do once or twice a week, like clean your room, brush the dog, and water the plants.

Mark each completed job with a star or other sticker. Surprise your child with a treat after he or she receives five or ten stickers.

The pencil pages that follow provide practice with initial and final digraphs. Digraphs most commonly appear at the beginning or at the end of words and come together to make a single new sound, like *sh*, *th*, and *ch*.

Help-Out Chart

Here are some different ways you might show when each project is to be done:

- Use check marks to show project days.

- Color the squares to show the difference between daily and weekly jobs.

- Add jobs for the whole family and write initials in the squares to show who will do the chores.

Check your plan after a week. Revise your plan, if needed.

	make bed	feed dog	trash day	clean room
Monday	✓	✓	✓	
Tuesday	✓	✓		✓
Wednesday	✓	✓		
Thursday	✓	✓		
Friday	✓	✓	✓	
Saturday	✓	✓		✓
Sunday	✓	✓	✓	

Beginning Digraphs

sh th ch

Name each picture and write the missing letters.

_____eese

_____oe

_____ermos

_____eep

_____erry

_____ip

_____irteen

Picture Names: *cheese, shoe, thermos, sheep, cherry, ship, thirteen*

Ending Digraphs

sh th ch

Name each picture and write the missing letters.

pea_____

di_____

bru_____

fi_____

tee_____

ben_____

mo_____

Picture Names: *dish, peach, brush, fish, teeth, bench, moth*

Playing Together

Down-the-Path Game

To play "Down-the-Path," you'll need a game board. Trace the pattern on the next page, or draw a game board on poster board.

- Draw a winding path and divide it into spaces, so they look like the sections of a sidewalk.

- Decorate the game board with drawings of things in your neighborhood, such as flowers, trees, homes, stores, or street signs.

Next, make the playing cards. Cut ten index cards in half. Write a consonant cluster or digraph you've learned on each. Place the cards face down in a pile near the game board.

Now, you're ready to play with a partner. Here's how:

- Place a marker, like a penny, at the start of the path.

- Pick a letter card. Say a word that begins with the letter pair. Move forward one space for each word you can name.

- When you can't name any more words, your partner takes a turn.

- Who gets to the end first?

As you play the game, note which consonant clusters and digraphs your child knows and which ones he or she needs more practice on. If more practice is needed, adapt "Gone Fishing," on page 36, to focus on specific clusters and digraphs.

Game Board

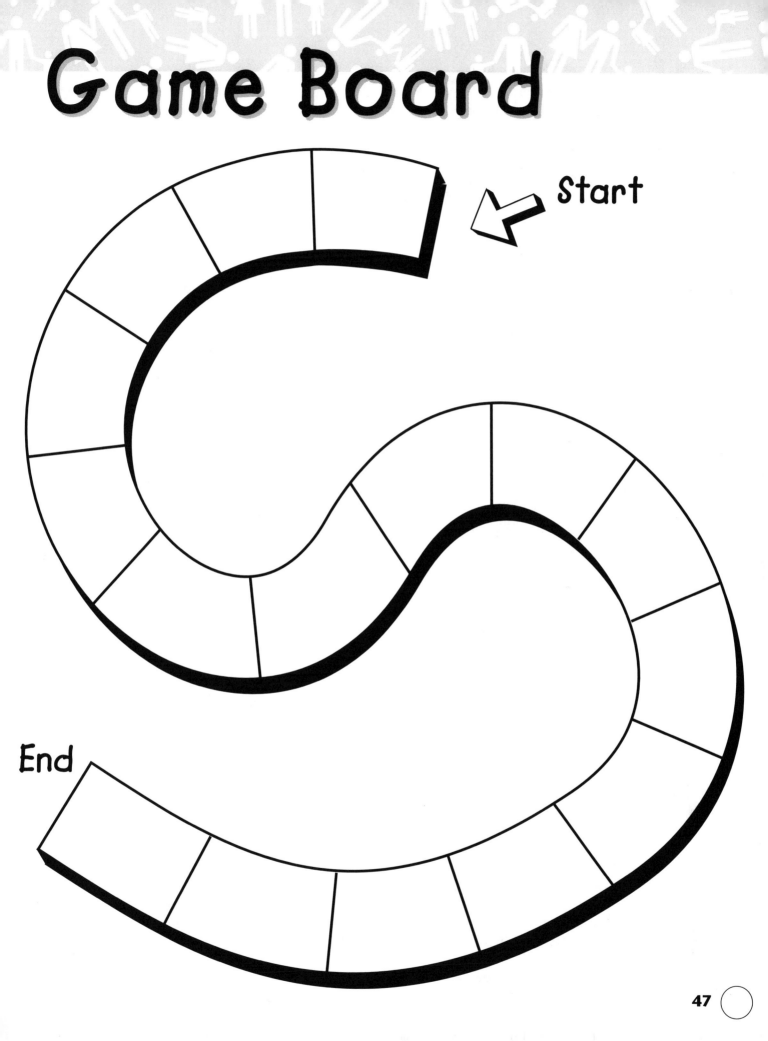

Start

End

Books to Share

Whether you prefer fact or fiction, human or animal characters, books about families abound in libraries and bookstores. Here are a few that you and your child might enjoy.

Five Minutes Peace by Jill Murphy (Putnam, 1986). An elephant mother wants some peace and quiet, but her three children always want her.

Clean Your Room, Harvey Moon by Pat Cummings (Macmillan, 1991). Harvey must tackle a Saturday chore before he can watch television. What's under the suspicious lumps in his rug?

Leo the Late Bloomer by Robert Kraus (Crowell, 1971). After a slow start, Leo the tiger surprises his worried father by blooming all at once.

I Know a Place by Karen Ackerman (Houghton, 1992). Warm illustrations help to convey the familiar feelings and comforts of home.

More books you might enjoy:

Come to the Meadow by Anna Grossnickle Hines (Houghton, 1984). A young girl's family is too busy for the delights of spring until Granny suggests having a picnic.

Fathers, Mothers, Sisters, Brothers: A Collection of Family Poems by Mary Ann Hoberman (Little, 1991). This rhyming anthology celebrates all kinds of families.

Noisy Nora by Rosemary Wells (Dial, 1997). New, full-color art updates this 1973 classic about Nora who, feeling neglected, makes more and more noise to attract her parents' attention.

Titch by Pat Hutchins (Macmillan, 1971). The youngest in the family, Titch has the smallest of everything until he plants a seed that grows and grows.

Suggestions

Invite your child to read aloud the story on the next page. If necessary, remind your child to think about letter sounds, picture clues, and what makes sense in the sentence as he or she reads.

✱ After reading the story, talk about the different ways these family members had fun together. Then invite your child to draw and write about a fun time he or she has shared with a family member. Your child can use the language pattern from the story. For example: *"I have fun with my uncle. We read together."*

We Have Fun Together

"I have fun with my mom," said Joey. "We jump together."

"I have fun with my dad," said Monkey. "We swing together."

"I have fun with my brother," said Duck. "We swim together."

"I have fun with my sister," said Bear. "We fish together."

4

"I have fun with my family,"
said Possum. "We hang
around together."

6

"I have fun with my _____," said _____ .

"We _____ together."

Animals in the Wild

CHAPTER 3

A Searching

A searching we will go,
A searching we will go,
We'll find a fish
And put it in a dish,
And then we'll watch it go.

Traditional

A Note About Animals in the Wild

Most children are fascinated by animals, especially wild ones. The activities in *Animals in the Wild* invite you and your child to explore the lives of wild animals—large and small, docile and fierce—while practicing these reading skills:

PHONICS/SHORT VOWELS: Most children begin to learn about vowel sounds and spellings in first grade. In *Animals in the Wild*, the spelling pattern CVC (Consonant-Vowel-Consonant) is used to introduce the short vowel sounds for *a, e, i, o,* and *u.*

PHONICS/SHORT VOWEL PHONOGRAMS: When learning the CVC pattern, first graders are usually introduced to short vowel phonograms (e.g., *-at*), or word families. Here, your child will recognize that if he or she can read a word, such as *cat,* he or she can also read *bat, fat, hat,* and so on.

PHONICS/DOUBLE FINAL CONSONANTS: First graders are usually able to decode words with double final consonants but may make errors when writing them by using a single final consonant. The double final consonants *ff, ll,* and *ss* are practiced in this chapter.

COMPARE/CONTRAST: One way in which children learn is to compare and contrast unfamiliar items with familiar ones. Encourage your child to compare and contrast any new animals he or she encounters with familiar ones. Suggest or supply vocabulary, such as *scales, tusk, antler, quill,* or *hoof,* that will aid in the comparisons.

FANTASY/REALISM: As you read stories or watch television programs together, talk about which animal characters or events are real and which are make-believe. Compare a fanciful animal character to its real counterpart.

In addition to making predictions and thinking about words (Chapters 1 and 2), young readers are learning to monitor their reading. *Monitoring* involves determining whether what is being read in a story makes sense and what to do if it doesn't. If something doesn't make sense, your child will learn to apply "fix-up" strategies, such as:

- reading again for information;
- looking at illustrations for help;
- asking for help.

Let's Go on a Safari

Have you ever gone on an animal safari? Maybe you've searched a park for rabbits or looked in the woods for deer. Well, here's how to go on safari, without leaving home!

Animal Binoculars

One handy item for a safari is binoculars. Here's how to make a pair from a paper towel tube:

- Ask a grownup to help you cut a paper towel tube in half.

- Staple the two halves together and paint or color designs on them.

- Punch two holes on the ends of the tubes and thread some yarn through them. Now you can hang the binoculars around your neck!

Sing a Safari Song

The poem at the chapter's beginning is also a singing game. Sing the words and then try making up more verses. Just think of animal names and rhyming words. Here are a few silly ideas to start you off:

- We'll find a bear and seat it in a chair ...
- We'll find a kangaroo and put it in a shoe ...
- We'll find a snake and offer it a cake ...

Wild Animal Map

Where do wild animals live? Some, like squirrels and rabbits, live in many places. Others, like hippos, kangaroos, and tigers, live in special parts of the world.

Seven Continents

The world map on the next page shows seven land masses called continents. Ask a grownup to help you read their names and the ocean names. Color light green the continent where you live and the oceans light blue. Color the other continents bright colors. Think about these questions as you color:

Which continent has water all around it?

What two continents are about the same size?

Which continent is the biggest? The smallest?

Now, let's find out where some wild animals live.

- Where does a kangaroo live? If you said Australia, you're right. Write **kangaroo** on a sticky note. Put it on the map near Australia and connect it with a line.

- Write **hippo** on a sticky note for the continent of Africa. **Zebras** and **lions** also live in Africa.

- Add a sticky note for **tiger** near Asia. There are also **elephants** in Asia.

As you learn more about wild animals and where they live, add their names to the map.

You may wish to photocopy the map on page 55 and paste it onto a larger sheet of paper. Pictures of animals can then be pasted around the border and connected to the continents where the animals live.

World Map

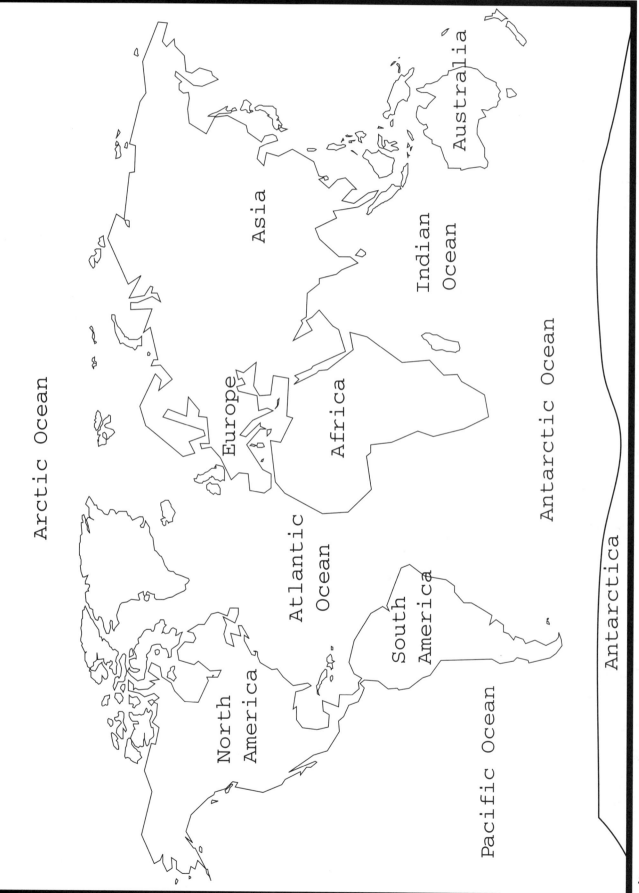

Australia

Asia

Indian
Ocean

Arctic Ocean

Europe

Africa

Antarctic Ocean

Atlantic
Ocean

North
America

South
America

Antarctica

Pacific Ocean

Discover Wild Animals

What are wild animals? They're animals that aren't kept in homes or on farms. Wild animals can live any place. You can learn more about wild animals with these projects.

Neighborhood Watch

Go on an animal hunt in your neighborhood, and list the animals you see. Are there cats and dogs? Squirrels and rabbits? Raccoons? Deer? What other animals live in your area? Add these animals to your list. Ask a grownup for help. Save the list for the next activity.

Neighborhood Drawing

Use your "Neighborhood Watch" list to plan an animal drawing. Here's how:

- Draw a line down the middle of a sheet of paper. Write **Tame** on one side and **Wild** on the other.

- Decide if each animal is tame or wild. Then draw it under the correct heading.

Animal Adventure Album

Start a photo album of wild animals. Cut out animal pictures from magazines. Arrange the animals by where they live, (desert, plains, etc.), or how they travel (land, sea, or air). Then create your album:

- Glue the pictures for one animal group onto a sheet of paper. Label each picture.

- Design a cover for your album.

- Punch holes along one edge and lace the pages together with yarn.

Turn your neighborhood animal search into a game. See how many different wild animals you observe in your neighborhood during a week. Check out some library books about a few of these critters.

 # Animal Scene

What animal interests you? Why not learn more about it and where it lives? Ask a grownup to help you find a picture book about your critter at the library and then create its world in a shoebox. Here are some things you might include:

- Small stones, twigs, and grass make good wooded habitats.

- Cotton balls can be used for snowy landscapes.

- Plastic wrap looks wet and shiny for water scenes.

Don't forget your animal! It might be a drawing, a clay model, a tiny plastic toy, or a stuffed animal.

I'd Like to Be...

If you could be any wild animal in the world, what would you be? Would you pick a large animal like a whale or an elephant? Or, maybe you'd pick a small one, like a field mouse or a chipmunk. Draw a picture of the animal you'd choose, and write a few sentences about what you'd do if you were this animal.

Safari Munchies

 Looking for wild animals can work up an appetite. Try one or more of these recipes to chase away your hunger.

Desert Trail Mix

Here's a make-and-take snack for your next outdoor walk:

- Put 2 tablespoons of raisins in a bowl.

- Add 1 tablespoon each of peanuts, sunflower seeds, shredded coconut, mini chips, or bite-size snacks, like dried cereal or pretzels.

- Mix together and enjoy!

Rainforest Granola

Gather up these ingredients to make a healthy breakfast cereal. You'll need a grownup's help for this one:

2/3 cup rolled oats

1/4 cup shredded coconut

1/4 cup cashews

1/4 cup almonds

1/4 cup dried banana chips

1/4 cup brown sugar

1) Stir the oats, cashews, and almonds in a skillet over low heat for 5 minutes.

2) Add the coconut and banana chips. Stir for 5 minutes.

3) Add the brown sugar. Stir for 3 more minutes. Let cool.

Enjoy as a snack or with milk.

The activities on pages 59 and 60 practice short *a* and *e*. After completing them, your child can think of words in these families: *-ack, -ad, -an, -ed, -en, -ell.*

Short a and e

Name each picture. Write the letter that stands for the vowel sound.

c _a_ t

b _e_ d

m ___ p

h ___ m

v ___ n

w ___ b

t ___ n

l ___ g

Picture Names: *cat, bed, map, ham, van, web, ten, leg*

Short a and e Families

Cat ends with **at**. Jet ends with **et**. Can you write the beginning letter or letters for other words in each family?

c a t

j e t

m

b

ch

g

n

___at

___at

___at

___at

___at

___et

___et

___et

___et

___et

Possible Responses: *cat: bat, brat, chat, hat, mat...; jet: bet, met, net, get, let...*

Animal Facts

How would you describe a bear to someone who had never seen one? Would you say it had four legs and fur? You can use an animal's features to describe it and compare it with other animals.

🕐 Animal Features

Look at the chart to find animal names and animal features. Now, point to the row that says **bear**. Which boxes have an **X** in them? The **X** shows that bears have 4 legs and fur. Put **X**'s in the chart to tell about the other animals. You can also make your own chart for different animals.

	0 legs	2 legs	4 legs	feathers	fur	scales
bear			X		X	
duck						
lion						
fish						

Your child can add more features to the chart, such as *hard shell, quills,* or *eight legs.* Or, you might create charts to tell about animal diets (meat, fish, plants, fruits, nuts) or habitats.

Animal Fun

You can use all that you now know about wild animals to make up animal riddles!

🕐 Riddles to Solve

Before you write your own riddles, try these:

I have four legs and am covered in fur.
I live in a cave and love to eat honey.
I'm also very good at climbing trees.
What am I? bear

I have two legs, and I run very fast.
I have wings, but I cannot fly.
I am one of the biggest birds in the world.
What am I? ostrich

The activities on pages 63 and 64 practice short *i*, *o*, and *u*. After your child completes page 64, encourage him or her to think of other words in these short vowel word families: *-in*, *-ing*, *-ock*, *-og*, *-ump*, *-ut*.

🕐 Creating Riddles

Now that you've solved some animal riddles, try to write a few of your own. Your riddle should give clues that describe your animal. The clues might tell what the animal looks like, what it eats, where it lives, or an interesting fact. You could even give a clue that compares your animal with another animal, like this: "I look like a horse, but I have stripes."

"What am I?" zebra

Short i, o, and u

Name each picture. Write the letter that stands for the vowel sound.

b _u_ s

b _o_ x

p _i_ g

s ___ x

p ___ t

c ___ p

b ___ g

p ___ n

m ___ p

Picture Names: *bus, box, pig, six, pot, cup, bug, pin, mop*

Short i, o, and u Families

Look at the word endings. Can you name and write the beginning letter for other words in each family?

c o t

p i g

___ o t

___ o t

b u g

___ i g   b

___ o t   p   ___ u g

___ i g

___ o t   ___ u g

___ i g   f

j   ___ u g

___ i g

___ u g

h   g   d

Possible Responses: *pig: big, dig, fig, wig...; cot: dot, got, hot, jot...; bug: dug, hug, jug, mug...*

Creepy Crawler Fun

There are plenty of wild creatures that aren't big. In fact, thousands of these wild critters are very, very small. Some even live in your own backyard. You guessed it! They're bugs.

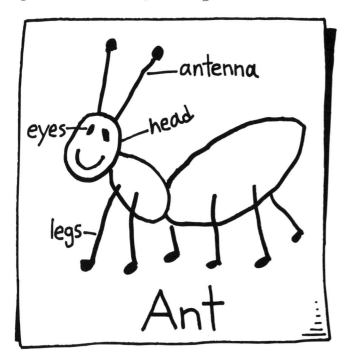

Ant

Buggy Poster

Pick a favorite bug or one you want to learn more about to show on a poster. Find out more about this bug by watching it in real life or by looking in books. On your poster, write words and draw pictures to share what you learn. You might show these things:

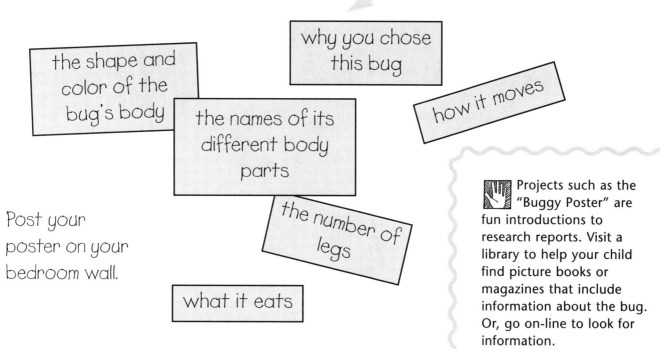

why you chose this bug

the shape and color of the bug's body

the names of its different body parts

how it moves

the number of legs

Post your poster on your bedroom wall.

what it eats

Projects such as the "Buggy Poster" are fun introductions to research reports. Visit a library to help your child find picture books or magazines that include information about the bug. Or, go on-line to look for information.

Animal Words

You've learned a lot about animals. You know their names. You know what they look like and where they live. But did you know that there are special words to name baby animals? Check it out.

Animal Babies

What is a baby dog called? A baby cat? Did you say **puppy** and **kitten**? Look at the list to learn some other baby animal names.

Think about farm animals and pets whose young are called **pup**, **calf**, **chick**, **colt**, and **kit**. Can you circle these animals on the list?

Animal Concentration

Make word cards for the names of adult animals and their young. Then use the cards to play a memory game, like "Kitchen Concentration" on page 26. Try to match adult and young animal names.

Adult	Young
bear	cub
beaver	kit
deer	fawn
elephant	calf
fox	pup
giraffe	calf
goose	gosling
kangaroo	joey
ostrich	chick
seal	pup
whale	calf
zebra	colt

CVC (consonant-vowel-consonant) words usually have a short vowel sound, a generalization that includes words that begin or end with clusters or digraphs, such as *flat*, *that*, *path*, and *past*, and those that end with double consonants, as on the following pencil page.

Double Final Consonants

Some words end in double consonants. Write **ff, ll,** or **ss** to complete each word.

dre _____

cu _____

hi _____

gla _____

be _____

do _____

Picture Names: *dress, cuff, hill, glass, bell, doll*

Animal Match-Up

A zebra with a bear's head? A rabbit with the body of a skunk? What kind of game is this? Read on to find out.

◑ The Game Cards

Before you can play this game, you'll need to make game cards. Begin by listing at least ten wild animals you want to include in the game. Then draw each animal on an index card. Next, cut out each card so the head is on one card and the body is on the other. Divide the cards into two piles: heads and bodies. Shuffle each pile.

◕ The Rules

With a grownup, make up rules for your "Animal Match-Up" game. These questions can help you:

- Should players start off with a few cards, or should each player take turns drawing cards?

- What happens when players make a match? Do they get an extra turn?

- How many matches must a player make to win?

Follow your rules to play the game. Are there any rules you could change to make the game better?

Shuffle the cards to make an unusual creature match. Take turns making up names for the new creature and telling a story about it. On another day, encourage your child to write and illustrate a story about one of the mismatched creatures.

In order for the animal cards to match up as neatly as possible, pencil off where the neck appears on each head and body. In this way, odd matches will still produce interesting, yet "put together," creatures.

Look at all the things I can do!

☐ I can say and write the letters of the alphabet.

☐ I can read words I do not recognize by thinking about:

  ☐ beginning and ending consonant sounds;

  ☐ l sounds like **bl, cl, fl, gl, pl,** and **sl;**

  ☐ r sounds like **br, cr, dr, fr, gr, pr,** and **tr;**

  ☐ s sounds like **sc, sk, sl, sm, sn, sp, st,** and **sw;**

  ☐ sounds like **sh, th,** and **ch;**

  ☐ short vowel sounds;

  ☐ short vowel word families.

☐ I can sort things by thinking about their size, shape, color, or how they are used.

☐ I can tell how things are alike and different.

Books to Share

Animals are favorite topics in both fiction and nonfiction books. Here are some books—both old and new—you might want to share with your child. As you share each one, help your child decide if the story and characters are real or make-believe.

Quick as a Cricket by Audrey Wood (Child's Play, 1982). A little boy compares himself to all kinds of animals, expressing himself in similes.

Little Gorilla by Ruth Bornstein (Clarion, 1976). All the forest animals love Little Gorilla until he grows bigger and bigger. What happens now?

Animal Tracks by Arthur Dorros (Scholastic, 1991). Can you and your child name the animal tracks left by the forest stream? Turn the page to discover the source of each new set of tracks.

The Wildlife A-B-C: A Nature Alphabet Book by Jan Thornhill (Simon, 1988). Rhyming text and beautiful illustrations guide children through an alphabet of amazing wildlife.

*My Story Suggestions

Ask your child to read aloud the story on the next page and offer assistance as needed. Encourage your child to use what he or she knows about the sounds for letters and picture clues to read the words.

✳ After reading the story together, talk about the similes (e.g., "clever as a fox"). Ask why people think of lions as being brave, foxes as being clever, and mice as being quiet. Then invite your child to draw and write about what he or she would do if looking for animals in the woods. Your child might write an original sentence or use the language pattern from the story. For example: "*I will be as (silent) as a (clam).*"

More books you might enjoy:

A Walk in the Wild by Lorraine Ward (Charlesbridge, 1993). Learn how a wildlife refuge operates in this book about Arkansas National Wildlife Refuge in Texas.

Oh, A-Hunting We Will Go by John Langstaff (Houghton 1974). A variety of animal rhymes is presented in this version of the traditional song.

Watch Where You Go by Sally Noll (Greenwillow, 1990). A little mouse makes his way home without being aware of the danger he passes through.

Who Is the Beast? by Keith Baker (Harbrace, 1990). Who is the beast by the jungle pool? Find out as a host of animals flee from the thirsty beast.

Wild Animal Search

When we go searching for wild animals,

I will be as brave as a lion.

I will be as clever as a fox.

I will be as curious as a monkey.

And I will be as quiet as a mouse.

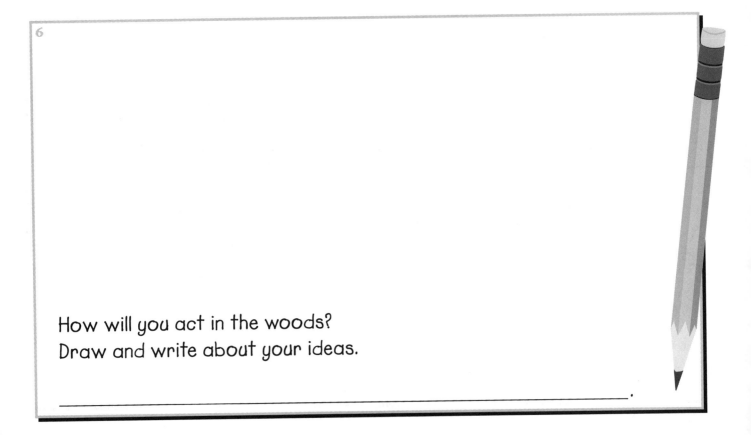

How will you act in the woods?
Draw and write about your ideas.

_____.

2

A Year of Seasons

Four Seasons

Spring is showery, flowery, bowery.

Summer: hoppy, croppy, poppy.

Autumn: wheezy, sneezy, freezy.

Winter: slippy, dippy, nippy.

Unknown

A Note About A Year of Seasons

For many children, seasonal changes are distinct. There's snow in the winter, rain in the spring, sun in the summer, and colorful foliage in the fall. For those in temperate climates, however, seasons may only be marked by changing holiday displays in store windows. *A Year of Seasons* invites you and your child to explore each season, wherever you may live, while practicing these reading skills:

PHONICS/LONG VOWELS: After learning about short vowels through the spelling pattern CVC (Consonant-Vowel-Consonant), most first graders are introduced to long vowel sounds. In this chapter, long vowel sounds for *a, i, o,* and *u* are introduced through the CVC*e* spelling pattern.

PHONICS/LONG VOWEL PAIRS: As children learn more about long vowel sounds, they are introduced to pairs of letters that can stand for a long vowel sound. In this chapter your child will practice the long vowel pairs *ai, ay, ea, ee, oa* and *ow.*

COMPOUND WORDS: Beginning readers often hesitate over big words but are delighted to find out that they can easily decode compound words. Here, your child will practice looking for the two words that make up a compound word.

MAKING GENERALIZATIONS: Seasonal generalizations tell us that winter is cold and snowy, while summer is hot and sunny. First graders are learning that they can make generalizations about the things they know and experience.

DRAWING CONCLUSIONS: Children venture beyond broad generalizations when they draw conclusions. Here, they are asked to use the information at hand along with their prior experience to come up with a conclusion. If someone enters the classroom carrying a dripping umbrella and wearing wet rain boots, for instance, classmates can conclude that it is raining outside. Encourage your child to draw conclusions as situations arise during the day as well as during shared reading time.

In addition to phonics and reading skills, a reading strategy children learn is *evaluating,* or making judgments about a story or a selection.

During and after reading a story, you might ask your child questions such as the following to help him or her evaluate what was read:
- Do you like the story? Why or why not?
- Does the book answer your questions?
- Did you learn anything new? What was it?

4

Four Seasons

Winter, spring, summer, fall. Each season is wonderful in its own way. How are the seasons special? Close your eyes and try to picture them, one at a time. Then make a list to tell how each season is special.

◑ A Four Seasons Box

You can use your list to create a "Four Seasons Box."

- First, find a box—like a shoe box or a tissue box—to decorate.

- Then cut pieces of construction paper the same size as the sides on the box.

- On each piece of paper, illustrate a different season. Use your list to help you decide what to draw.

- Glue your drawings to the box.

Now you have a "Four Seasons Box" to save reminders of the things you do during the year. Photographs, invitations, greeting cards, ticket stubs, or any other small souvenirs can go in here!

If your child needs help listing seasonal characteristics, suggest things people see or do in a season and have him or her name the season. If your seasons are not distinct, share generalizations such as fall colors and snowy winters.

Create a four seasons mural with your child. Divide a large sheet of paper into four sections and label them *winter, spring, summer,* and *fall.* Ask your child to draw or paste pictures in the appropriate section.

Twelve Months

You know that a year has four seasons and twelve months. Can you name the months in each season? Let's find out.

☽ The Starting Months

Divide a piece of paper into four sections. Write a season name in each section. Then write these starting months under the season shown.

- Winter begins in **December**.
- Spring begins in **March**.
- Summer begins in **June**.
- Fall begins in **September**.

Say and write the months in order to complete the chart. Then illustrate the seasons.

☁ My Own Calendar

If you make 12 copies of the next page, you can use the pages to create your own calendar.

- Write each month's name at the top of each page. Then ask a grownup to help you number the days on the calendar.

- Have fun decorating it! You can write in family birthdays and holidays and draw pictures for them.

Use your child's calendar to record special events, such as losing a tooth.

You may want to spread the calendar activity out over several days, or do one page per month.

Calendar Page

Year: _____

Month: _____

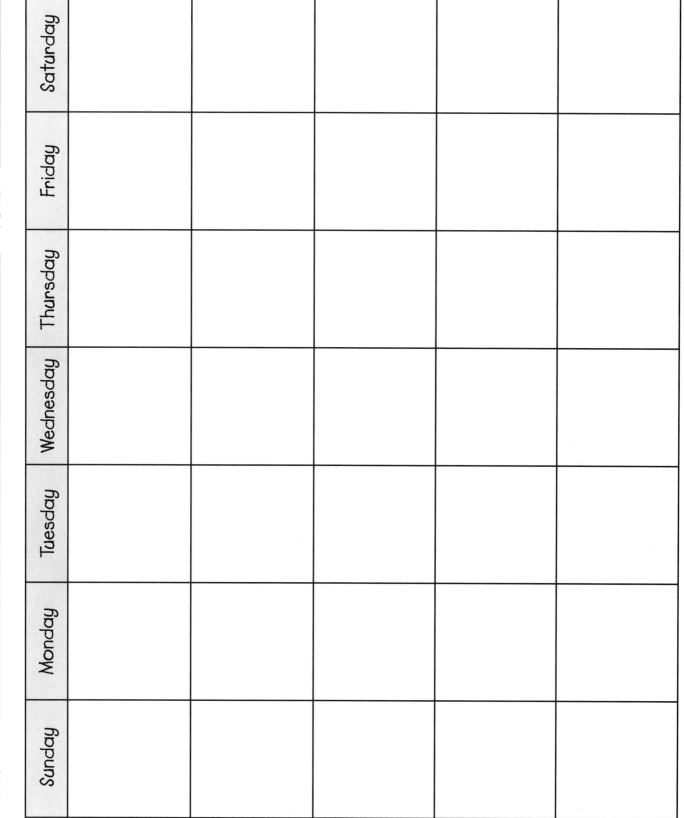

Sunday	Monday	Tuesday	Wednesday	Thursday	Friday	Saturday

Seasonal Drinks

A tasty drink is a treat in any season. Take your pick of the recipes below. Or, try all four! (Make sure you ask an adult to help you.)

Autumn Punch

This recipe celebrates the colors of fall and makes enough to serve your friends.

Combine in a large mixing bowl 1/2 gallon each of cranberry juice and apple cider. Mix in a 6-ounce can of thawed orange juice concentrate. Enjoy.

Hot Chocolate

Winter is a time for snowmen, sled rides, and hot chocolate.

Put a teaspoon or two of chocolate syrup or powder into a mug. Carefully add warm milk and stir. For an extra special hot chocolate, add a cinnamon or peppermint stick or sprinkle in a few marshmallows.

Sparkle Juice

Need a refreshing drink after a spring softball or soccer game? Try this:

Pour equal amounts of your favorite fruit juice and ginger ale (or club soda) into a tall glass of ice. Stir and drink.

Berry Freeze

Here's a drink that can help you cool off at the end of a hot summer day.

Put 1 cup milk, 1/2 cup of ice cubes, and 1/4 cup of strawberries into a blender. Blend until smooth. Then enjoy!

The pencil pages that follow practice the CVC*e* (Consonant-Vowel-Consonant-*e*) spelling pattern for the long *a, i, o,* and *u* vowel sounds. Your child will find this pattern in words like *game, time, home,* and *cube.*

Long a and i

Name the pictures. Write the letters that make each long vowel sound.

g a t e

k i t e

v _ s _

m _ c _

p _ p _

f _ c _

t _ p _

b _ k _

Picture Names: *gate, kite, vase, mice, pipe, face, bike, tape*

79

Long o and u

Name the pictures. Write the letters that make each long vowel sound.

r _o_ p _e_

m _u_ l _e_

c __ b __

b __ n __

t __ b __

fl __ t __

r __ s __

r __ b __

Picture Names: *mule, rope, cube, bone, tube, flute, rose, robe*

How Hot? How Cold?

What is the weather like during the seasons where you live? Are your winters coat-and-mitten weather or sweater weather? Does it snow? Or is it rainy and cold?

| Mon. | Tues. | Wed. | Thurs. | Fri. | Sat. | Sun. |

Whatever the Weather

Find out what kind of weather you have during the different seasons by keeping a weather chart. Set up your chart to look like a calendar, or use the calendar pattern on page 77.

As each day goes by, record the weather for that day by drawing a picture symbol. Can you tell what the picture symbols on this weather chart stand for?

If you have an outdoor thermometer, check the temperature at the same time each day and record it on your chart.

At the end of the month, look at your calendar. What can you say about the kind of weather your area usually has at this time of year?

Help your child find the weather map in the newspaper. Work together to answer these questions:

- Which part of the country is the hottest at this time of the year? The coldest?
- Which part gets the most rain or snow?
- Where would you like to visit?

Rainy Day Fun

Have you ever heard the phrase "April showers bring May flowers"? Well, it's true. Spring is usually a rainy time of year. But the rain and the warmer weather do help flowers and plants grow and bloom. In the meantime, what can you do on those rainy spring days? Here are two ideas.

Daisy Crazy

Plant daisy or other flower seeds in an egg carton. Water the soil lightly every other day. Keep a journal of the things you do and see. On which days do you water the soil? How long before the first seedling appears? What do the seedlings look like?

When the seedlings are about an inch or two tall, replant them in a pot. Or, if the weather's warm enough, plant them outside in a sunny spot.

Rainy Day Painting

On the next rainy day, use markers to draw a design on heavy paper. Then take the drawing outside and let a few raindrops hit the page. Bring the drawing back inside and wait for it to dry. Does anything about the drawing surprise you?

The following pencil page practices the long vowel *a* sound represented by the vowel pairs *ai* and *ay* as in *rainy* and *day*. After your child completes the page, have him or her look for these vowel pairs while reading and writing.

Long Vowel Pairs: ai, ay

Name the pictures. Then write the words by the matching numbers to complete the puzzle.

braid
chain   hay   gray
daisy   train   spray

ACROSS

1.

2.

3.

DOWN

4.

5.

6.

7.

Picture Names: *train, gray, daisy, braid, spray, chain, hay*

Trees and Leaves

What's the tallest living thing you've seen? A basketball player? A giraffe? A tree? Trees are living things, just like people. Take a closer look at trees and how they change.

◑ Autumn Leaves

Gather leaves that you think are especially colorful. Arrange them on wax paper. Then cover them with more wax paper. Ask a grownup to press the leaves and wax paper with a warm iron. Hang the pressed leaves in a window.

◔ Summer Leaf Rubbings

Go on a walk to collect leaves with different shapes. At home, put the leaves on a table and place a sheet of drawing paper over them. Gently rub a crayon over the leaves and the paper to make the rubbings.

Adopt a Tree

Pick a tree to call your own. It can be anywhere, as long as it's close enough to visit often. Observe how your tree changes from month to month and season to season. Draw pictures and keep a journal of the changes.

- When do new leaves grow?
- Does your tree have flowers? How about fruit?
- When do the leaves change color?
- How else does your tree change?

Lightweight paper, such as tissue or tracing paper, works best for leaf rubbings. When pressing leaves, place a handkerchief over the wax paper to keep the iron clean.

The following pencil page practices the long *e* sound represented by *ee* and *ea* as in *tree* and *leaf*. If your child needs help unscrambling the letters, suggest writing the vowel pair first and then the beginning and/or ending consonants.

Long Vowel Pairs: ee, ea

Name each picture. Then unscramble the letters to write the word.

b e a d
abde

aemt

east

reet

elsa

eshep

efet

Picture Names: *bead, meat, seat, tree, seal, sheep, feet*

85

What Do I Wear?

A coat, boots, mittens, and a hat—can you guess the time of year? Yes, it's winter! Here's a "What Do I Wear?" game that looks at clothes by the season.

◐ Create Game Cards

To play "What Do I Wear?" you'll need some game cards. First, list at least four articles of clothing for each season. When your list is complete, write the words on index cards and illustrate the cards. Then find a family member to play the game with you.

◕ Playing the Game

Place the playing cards face down on a table top and mix them up. To play the game, do this:

- Take turns choosing a card and looking at it.

- Try to decide if you'd wear the item in the winter, spring, summer, fall, or more than one season.

- Players keep drawing cards until someone makes a three-card set of items from one season. Then, begin again.

You may be surprised by some of the clothes your child links to a season. Ask your child to explain his or her reasoning. After all, many people do wear bathing suits in the winter, especially if they're heading to the gym for a swim.

The following pencil page practices the vowel pairs *oa* and *ow* as in *coat* and *snow*. As needed, help your child complete the first item.

Long Vowel Pairs: oa, ow

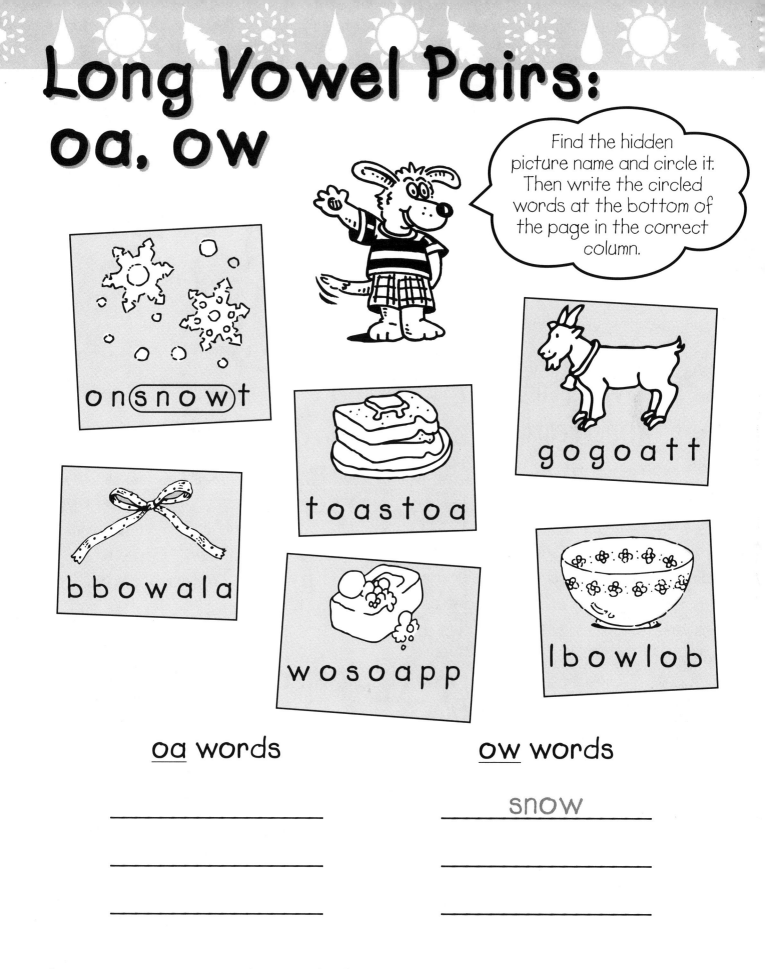

Find the hidden picture name and circle it. Then write the circled words at the bottom of the page in the correct column.

on s n o w t

g o g o a t t

t o a s t o a

b b o w a l a

w o s o a p p

l b o w l o b

oa words

_____

_____

_____

ow words

snow

_____

_____

Picture Names: *snow, toast, goat, bow, soap, bowl*

Word Play

What's the best season for fun and games? Any season! You can enjoy these word play games all year long.

🕐 Vowel Pair Word Families

Cut out raindrop shapes. Write a vowel pair word family on each raindrop: **ain, ay, eat, eed, oat, ow**. Then put the raindrops in a bucket. Pick one, like **ain**, and see how many words you can name for this family. Don't forget to try different beginning consonants (e.g., **cheat, chain, snow**).

🕐 Name-a-Compound

Write a compound word, such as **seaweed**, on a piece of paper and draw a line between the two words in it. Can you name any other compound words that use **sea** and **weed**? With a grownup, list as many words as you can. Then play the game with another compound word.

🕐 Vowel Magic

Words like **hop** have a short vowel pattern. Words like **hope** have a long vowel pattern with an **e** at the end. The next time you read a storybook, look for these kinds of words.

Cut out some mitten shapes and write the words **kite, cane, care,** and **mope** on the cutouts. Make sure you write the final **e** on the thumb of the mitten. You can then open and close the thumb to read a short and a long vowel word. How many words did you find?

Compound Words

Write the word that names each picture. Draw a line between the two words in the compound word.

waterfall
watermelon

water/melon

handshake
handstand

_____

toothpaste
toothbrush

_____

bedroom
bedspread

_____

sandbox
sandpaper

_____

seaweed
seashell

_____

Books to Share

In many picture books, the seasons play a major role in the story line. The following titles are examples of how important specific seasons can be. As you share the books, help your child make generalizations about the seasons and draw conclusions about characters and events.

What's the Matter with Carruthers? by James Marshall (Houghton, 1972). Emily Pig and Eugene become worried as the passing fall days turn a congenial bear, Carruthers, into a grouch. What is wrong?

A Turkey for Thanksgiving by Eve Bunting (Clarion, 1991). Mr. and Mrs. Moose invite all their animal friends for Thanksgiving dinner, but Turkey doesn't show up.

Make Way for Ducklings by Robert McCloskey (Viking, 1941). This Caldecott Award winner tells the story of Mr. and Mrs. Mallard and their search for a place to hatch their ducklings and raise a family.

Keep Looking by Millicent Selsam and Joyce Hunt (Macmillan, 1989). At first, these watercolor scenes of a farm house look empty, but closer observation reveals wild animals amid winter scenes.

*My Story Suggestions

Invite your child to read aloud the story on the next page and offer assistance as needed. Ask your child to draw conclusions to tell what season is shown in each frame.

✱ After your child has finished the story, talk about the ways in which the puppy and the seasons changed. For the last frame, ask your child to draw and write about something he or she likes to do during a particular time of year. Or, your child might want to draw and write a new story frame for Showers.

More books you might enjoy:

Chicken Soup with Rice by Maurice Sendak (Harper, 1962). Twelve seasonal verses extol the virtues of chicken soup with rice.

The Jacket I Wear in the Snow by Shirley Neitzel (Greenwillow, 1989). A young girl names all the clothes she wears in the snow.

Miss Rumphius by Barbara Cooney (Viking Penguin, 1982). With a handful of lupine, Miss Rumphius makes the world more beautiful.

The Pumpkin Patch by Elizabeth King (Dutton, 1990). A photoessay of a commercial patch from preparation of the soil to the fall harvest.

Showers's Year

1

New leaves, new flowers,
My new puppy's name is Showers.

2

Hot sun, lazy days,
Showers loves to swim and play.

3

Red, gold, orange, and yellow,
Showers is a funny fellow.

4

Cold winds, white snow,
Showers is always on the go!

5

Birthday bone, birthday cheer,
This has been Showers's year.

6

What do you like to do during the year?
Draw and write about your ideas.

_____.

Old Favorites

CHAPTER 5

The Gingerbread Man

Run, run as fast as you can.

You can't catch me

I'm the Gingerbread Man.

I ran from the woman.

I ran from the man.

And I can run from you!

Traditional

Old Favorites

Most reading programs devote some time to traditional tales. For many first graders, being able to read these familiar stories on their own marks them as readers. The activities in *Old Favorites* invite children to take a second look at their favorite tales and explore these reading skills:

PHONICS/SOUNDS FOR Y: After learning about long and short vowel sounds, first graders explore different vowel sounds and spellings. In *Old Favorites*, children practice the two vowel sounds for *y* as in *happy* and *fly*.

PHONICS/VOWEL PAIRS: Children begin to learn that the same letters can sometimes stand for different sounds, as with the vowel pair *oo* in *look* and *too*. They also practice alternate spellings for the vowel sound in *too—ou*, as in *soup*, *ew*, as in *flew*, and *ue*, as in *blue*.

PHONICS/r-CONTROLLED VOWELS: Another type of vowel sound is introduced in *Old Favorites*, the *r*-controlled vowels. Here the sounds for *ar*, as in *star*, and *or*, as in *corn*, are practiced.

PHONICS/BASE WORDS AND ENDINGS: In this chapter, your child will practice the plural endings *-s*, *-es*, and *-ies*; the comparative endings *-er* and *-est*; and the inflected endings *-ed* and *-ing*. Also, three suffixes *-y*, as in *snowy*, *-ly*, as in *slowly*, and *-ful*, as in *helpful*, are introduced.

FANTASY/REALISM: Often, traditional tales are so familiar to children, it is hard for them to distinguish what is fantasy and what is real. As you share these stories together, talk about the real and fanciful aspects of the setting, the events, and, most important, the characters.

STORY STRUCTURE: As children are exposed to more books, they learn that stories have many common parts. Help your child recognize common parts, such as setting, characters, and plot, by asking questions like these:

- Where does the story take place?
- Who is in the story?
- What happens in the story?

In the preceding chapters, we've identified strategies that help young readers to understand and enjoy what they read. One strategy that helps to check children's understanding is *summarizing*. Here, young readers use what they know about story structure to tell, in their own words, what a selection is about.

Be a Storyteller

Do you have a favorite folk tale or fairy tale? Is it "The Three Little Pigs"? How about "Goldilocks and the Three Bears"? Gather your family and friends together to tell them your favorite story.

🕐 Practice Makes Perfect

Once you decide on a story, read it again to help you remember the important parts. Then practice telling it. Here are some ideas to help you practice:

- What will your characters sound like? Plan a different voice for each one.

- What actions or facial expressions can you use to show that characters are happy, surprised, or scared?

- Will you use sound effects in your retelling?

- Think about what happens first, next, and last as you practice telling your story.

🕐 Tell the Story

Now you're ready to be a storyteller. Call together your friends and family. Have everyone make themselves comfortable. Then tell your tale in a loud clear voice.

Have a storytelling night. Let each member of the family retell a favorite folk or fairy tale.

Have your child summarize the story he or she wishes to tell. As needed, read the story again to help your child recall important details.

Storytellers use their own words to retell stories. Share versions of "The Three Little Pigs" by authors such as James Marshall, Erik Blegvad, and Paul Galdone. Share also regional variations, such as "The Three Little Hawaiian Pigs and the Magic Shark" by Donivee Martin Laird and "Los Tres Pequenos Jabalies: The Three Little Javelinas" by Susan Lowell. Or, read the parody, "The True Story of the Three Little Pigs" by Jon Scieszka, in which the wolf tells *his* side of the story.

Old Favorite Puppet Show

What is an old favorite? It's a folk or fairy tale that has been told for many years. Pick another old favorite to perform as a puppet show. Then gather your family and friends once more for a performance.

Spoon Puppets

Make a puppet for each character in your favorite "old favorite." Think about what each character looks like. Use markers to draw faces on the bowls of large plastic spoons. Then add yarn for hair and bits of fabric for clothes.

The Puppet Theater

Use a large cardboard box to make a puppet theater. Ask a grownup to help you cut off the top of the box and one of its sides. Decorate the other three sides any way you wish. You might cover them with shelf paper and draw pictures of your favorite folk and fairy tales.

Little Red Riding Hood

Act It Out

Use your puppets and theater to act out your favorite story for family and friends.

While most folk and fairy tales have happy endings, endings for the antagonist are seldom good. You may wish to preview several versions of stories such as "Little Red Riding Hood" for a version you feel is appropriate for your child.

The following pencil page practices two vowel sounds for the letter y, long e as in happy and long i as in fly. In decoding these words in context, ask your child to try both sounds for y to read the word.

A Happy Ending

Read the words. Then draw a line to follow the words with the same **y** sound that is in the word **happy**.

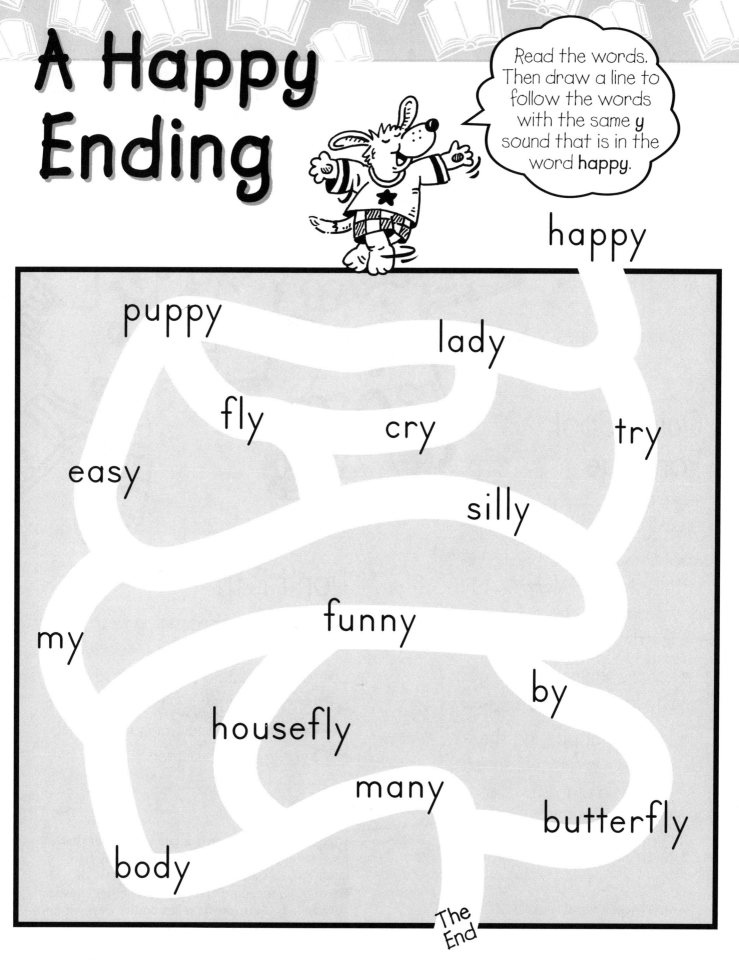

happy

puppy

lady

fly   cry   try

easy

silly

my

funny

by

housefly

many

butterfly

body

The End

Answers: *happy, lady, puppy, easy, silly, funny, body, many*

Old Favorite Recipes

How will the Three Bears make their next batch of porridge? What did Little Red Riding Hood really have in her basket? Try these recipes to find out.

Quick-Cool Porridge

The Three Bears went for a walk so their porridge could cool. But after what happened with Goldilocks, Mama Bear has decided to try this quick-cool recipe the next time she cooks.

- Follow the recipe for your favorite oatmeal mix.

- Instead of putting the oatmeal in a bowl, spread it onto a plate to cool more quickly.

- Pour a tiny bit of milk or syrup on top and sprinkle with cinnamon and sugar.

Don't Eat!

Here's a Gingerbread Boy that won't run away from you. Use a cookie cutter to trace a gingerbread boy shape on cardboard. Then cut it out. Decorate the gingerbread boy with markers, paint, or glitter.

Other tales: There's a tale even older than Grimm's *Rapunzel.* Compiled nearly two hundred years ago is the Neapolitan story of *Petrosinella,* meaning "parsley." While the tales start out similarly, Petrosinella relies on her own wit and courage to escape the tower and the ogress who keeps her.

Little Red's No-Bake Cookies

Little Red Riding Hood isn't allowed to use the stove by herself, so she likes to make these no-bake cookies. Here's the recipe:

1 cup granola

2 to 3 tablespoons honey

1 cup peanut butter

1/2 cup uncooked, rolled oats

2 tablespoons milk

1/2 cup powdered milk

Mix all the ingredients together. Then roll the dough into bite-size balls. Either chill the cookies in the refrigerator or eat them at room temperature.

Adapt a favorite recipe to go along with a favorite story. These questions might spark a few ideas: What did the Tortoise drink after his race with the Hare? What kind of salad would Rapunzel enjoy? What kind of house did Hanzel and Gretel see in the forest?

The pencil pages that follow practice vowel sounds for *oo*, as in *good* and the vowel pairs *ew, ou, ue,* and *oo,* as in *blew, soup, blue,* and *too.*

Stone Soup and a Story

You'll need these ingredients:

1 stone (optional; but if used, wash it well)

2 cans of tomato soup

2 cans of water

1/4 cup dry barley

2-3 cups of your favorite fresh vegetables (peas, string beans, carrots, corn, celery)

Wash the vegetables and ask a grownup to cut them into bite-size pieces. Then heat all the ingredients together in a large pot or saucepan until the vegetables are soft (about 20 minutes).

While you're waiting, read "Stone Soup." Many versions can be found in your library. When the soup is done, remove the stone and serve.

Two Sounds for oo

Write **oo** to complete the words under the pictures. Then write the words with the same vowel sound under **too** or **took**.

b o o k

b_____t

p_____l

w_____d

t_____th

h_____k

too

took

b o o k

_____

_____

_____

_____

_____

100

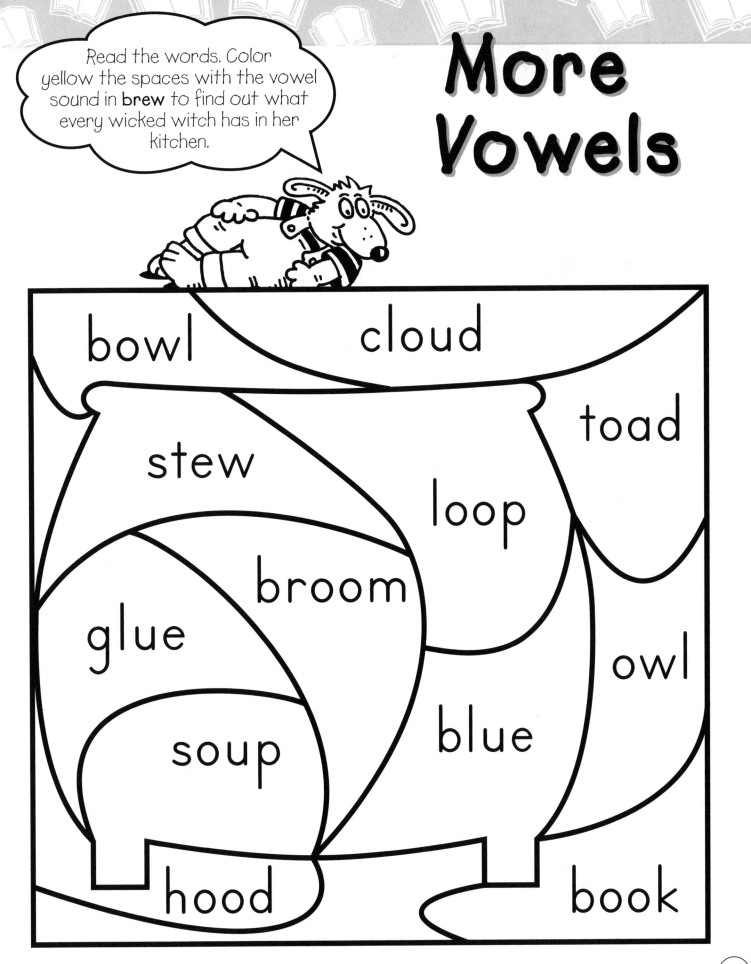

Read the words. Color yellow the spaces with the vowel sound in **brew** to find out what every wicked witch has in her kitchen.

More Vowels

bowl

cloud

toad

stew

loop

broom

glue

owl

blue

soup

hood

book

Answer: a kettle

Old Tales Map

Where did Little Red Riding Hood's grandmother live? How about the Three Bears? The Three Little Pigs? You decide, by making an "Old Tales Map."

◑ List the Neighbors

Plan the map. Decide which characters you want to include. Make a list to keep track of your ideas. Here are a few to get you started:

- house for Goldilocks; house for the Three Bears

- straw house, stick house, brick house for each Little Pig; a house for the Wolf

- house for Little Red Riding Hood; one for her grandma

- cottage in the glen for Sleeping Beauty; the king's palace; a witch's castle

Little Pig Lane

straw house

stick house

brick house

☁ Design the Map

On poster board or a large sheet of paper, decide where you'll put each character's home. Draw the homes. You might also add these features:

- woods or a forest

- a river or a lake

- paths through the woods or another road

- a mountain or a hill

Use the map to make up new stories for the characters.

✋ Your child can cut open and tape together paper grocery bags to make a map surface. As needed, help your child label the paths and homes. Encourage your child to think of other characters that might be on the map. For example, the tortoise from "The Tortoise and the Hare" might live in a creek and the hare might live in a burrow under a tree.

Vowels with r

Name each picture. Then write **ar** or **or** to complete the word.

st_____

th_____n

sh_____k

p_____ch

b_____n

c_____

c_____n

f_____k

Picture Names: *star, thorn, shark, porch, barn, car, corn, fork*

103

Book of Threes

Many old tales share a special number. Can you guess what it is? It's the number three. It's easy to find in the titles "Three Little Pigs" and "Three Billy Goats Gruff." You'll need your thinking cap to name others. Try it!

Story Title	Magic Number Three
Three Little Pigs	three pigs; three houses
Aladdin	Genie gives three wishes
Rumpelstiltskin	three chances to guess name
Sleeping Beauty	three fairies

🕐 Chart Folk & Fairy Tales

Make a chart of different folk and fairy tales you know. On the chart, write the story title and tell how the number three is shown. Your chart might look like the one above.

List as many different stories as you can. Then choose six stories for the next project.

🕐 A Book of Threes

Fold three sheets of white paper in half. Then staple the sheets along the fold to make a booklet. Write the title "Book of Threes" on the cover. On each page, write the title of a "three" story and draw a picture to show the threes.

Need some more ideas? Consider the boy who cried "wolf" three times, Cinderella's three stepsisters, the three princes in the *Frog Princess*, and the three magic acorns in *Petrosinella*.

Groups of three are good for practicing comparative and superlative (e.g. *big, bigger, biggest*) endings. After your child completes the following pencil page, help him or her identify the base words and the endings.

Base Words & Endings

Complete the sentences. Then write the words by the matching numbers to complete the puzzle.

biggest

pigs

chances

fairies

smaller

wishes

ACROSS

1. The Genie gave Aladdin three _____.

2. The Wolf huffed and puffed in this story about three _____.

3. Sleeping Beauty was cared for by three _____.

DOWN

4. The third Billy Goat Gruff was the _____ of the three.

5. Mama Bear was _____ than Papa Bear; Baby Bear was the smallest of all.

6. The Princess had three _____ to guess Rumpelstiltskin's name.

We Love a Happy Ending

Most folk and fairy tales have happy endings—for the good characters anyway. For other characters, the endings aren't always happy. How would you like to change the ending of a story so that everyone can be happy?

Name Unhappy Endings

Begin a list of stories with unhappy endings. List as many unhappy endings as you can. Here are a few ideas to start:

- Gingerbread boy gets eaten by fox.

- Baby Bear's favorite chair is broken.

- Cat, Duck, and Dog don't get to share the Little Red Hen's bread. (They also don't help the Little Red Hen!)

- The Three Little Pigs cook the Wolf in a big pot of water.

Rewrite an Ending

Now read through your list. Pick a story ending you'd like to rewrite. How could you change things so that everyone has a happy ending? Write your new ending. You may wish to draw pictures to go along.

Your child may wish to rewrite the entire story to reflect his or her happy ending. In this case, you may wish to have the story dictated to you for your child to illustrate.

"The Gingerbread Boy" is the American version of a story told around the world. In England the character is known as Johnny Cake. The Norse have a different runaway character in a story called "The Pancake." Russia's version is known as "The Bun."

More Base Words & Endings

Find the hidden word to complete each sentence. Circle the word, and then write it.

1. Little Red Riding Hood was _____ walking _____ to Grandma's house.

   w a (w a l k i n g) g

2. She was very _____ when she saw the Wolf.

   s c a r e d f u l e

3. Little Red Riding Hood _____ walked away.

   b i s q u i c k l y

4. But that old Wolf was _____.

   h a t t r i c k y d

5. He _____ up as Little Red's grandma.

   c h d r e s s e d s

6. Can you tell what _____ next?

   h a p p e n s l l y

What If?

What if Cinderella were a boy? What if Cinderella didn't wear glass slippers or go to a ball? How would the story be the same? Different?

Think About It

Sometimes the idea for a new story comes from an old one. In fact, there's a funny movie called **Cinderfella**, where Cinderella is a boy. In the book **Cinder-Elly**, by Frances Minters, a girl wears glass sneakers to a basketball game at school (instead of a ball at the palace).

Make your own list of "What If?" questions about favorite stories. Use the list to get ideas for a new story. Write down some of your ideas.

What if Cinderella's garden grew cucumbers instead of pumpkins?

Be an Author

• Choose one idea and use it to write a new story. Dictate the story to a family member. Then work together to read the story again and make changes.

• When you're pleased with your story, copy it neatly onto lined paper. Draw pictures to go with it. Then bind the pages together to make a book.

By the end of first grade, most teachers are using a four- or five-step writing process with children: prewriting (brainstorming ideas), drafting (rough draft), revising and/or proofreading, and publishing.

Cinderella is one of the most widely told stories in the world. In addition to the Russian Vasilisa, you might compare *Tattercoats* by Margaret Greaves (English), *Yeh-Shen*, by Ai-Ling Louie (Japanese), *The Egyptian Cinderella* by Shirley Climo, and *The Rough Face Girl* by Rafe Martin (Native American).

Look at all the things I can do!

- [ ] I can say and write the letters of the alphabet.
- [ ] I can read words I don't recognize by thinking about:
  - [ ] beginning and ending consonant sounds;
  - [ ] sounds with **r, l,** and **s;**
  - [ ] the sounds for **sh, th,** and **ch;**
  - [ ] the patterns for short vowels and long vowels;
  - [ ] the long vowel pairs **ai, ay, ea, ee, oa,** and **ow;**
  - [ ] the vowel pairs **oo, ou, ew,** and **ue;**
  - [ ] vowel plus **r** words;
  - [ ] compound words and base words with endings.
- [ ] I can think about story information and what I already know to draw conclusions.
- [ ] I can tell what happens in the beginning, in the middle, and at the end of a story.

Books to Share

You and your child can explore several retellings of a folk or fairy tale from different countries and cultures. This list starts you off with anthologies of popular tales and provides a multicultural sampling.

The Fairy Tale Treasury collected by Virginia Haviland (Dell, 1980). These 32 beloved stories range from the simple Henny Penny to the complex Snow White.

Lon Po Po retold and illustrated by Ed Young (Philomel, 1989). This Chinese version of Little Red Riding Hood is filled with danger and courage.

Foolish Rabbit's Big Mistake by Rafe Martin (Putnam, 1985). This retelling is the Jataka precursor of the Chicken Little and Henny Penny stories.

Baba Yaga and Vasilisa the Brave by Mariana Mayer (Morrow, 1994). This retelling of a Russian Cinderella story has the lovely Vasilisa confronting the witch Baba Yaga.

Anthologies of tales from around the world include:

Nursery Tales Around the World by Judy Sierra (Charlesbridge, 1993). Eighteen thematically grouped stories from international folklore.

Folktales and Fables of the World by Barbara Hayes & Robert Ingpen (Portland, 1987). A comprehensive collection of international tales.

The People Could Fly: American Black Folktales told by Virginia Hamilton (Knopf, 1985). Among these retold tales are several "Brer Animal" stories.

The Maid of the North & Other Folk Tale Heroines by Ethel Johnston Phelps (Holt, 1983). A gathering of resourceful heroines from seventeen cultures.

*My Story Suggestions

Read aloud the story on the next page with your child. Point out, if your child does not, that this story is a retelling of a fable. Mention that fables are stories that teach lessons.

✱ After reading the story, ask your child how this retelling of the Tortoise and the Hare might be different from or similar to other versions. Then invite your child to draw and write about the fable's lesson in the last frame.

Turtle and Rabbit

"Turtle," said Rabbit, "you move so slowly. How do you ever get anywhere?"

"I get there soon enough," said Turtle. "And I'll race you to prove it."

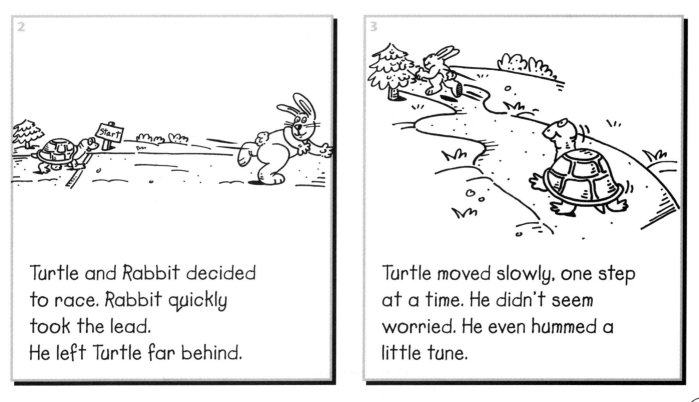

Turtle and Rabbit decided to race. Rabbit quickly took the lead. He left Turtle far behind.

Turtle moved slowly, one step at a time. He didn't seem worried. He even hummed a little tune.

4

Rabbit ran so quickly that he grew very tired. He curled up to take a nap under a tree. While Rabbit napped, Turtle rounded the bend.

5

Step by step, Turtle passed Rabbit. Step by step, Turtle crossed the finish line. The cheering animals woke up Rabbit. But, it was too late. Turtle had won.

6

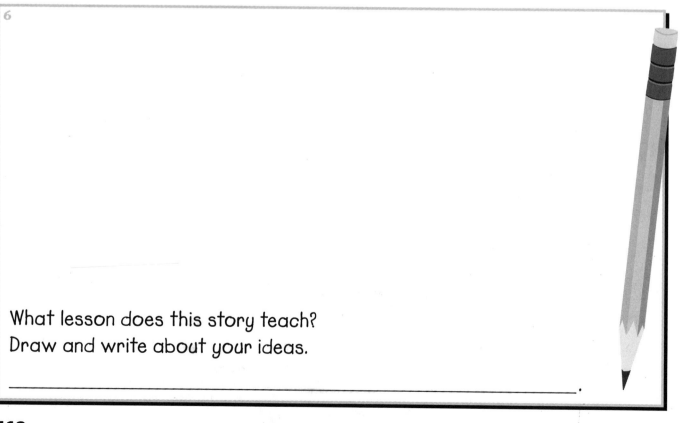

What lesson does this story teach? Draw and write about your ideas.

_____